The Galloping Garbage Truck

The Galloping Garbage Truck

Poems by

Pamela R. Anderson-Bartholet

Cover art and Illustrations by R.E. Anderson

ISBN: 978-1-954353-71-8

Kelsay Books
502 South 1040 East, A-119
American Fork, Utah, 84003

Dedicated to

Daniel, Fallon, Finn, Guthrie, Leah, Oliver, and Peter

Contents

Buttons

Matching buttons down my front.
From neck to waist they stitch me up.

But wondering I'm prone to do
about the need to twin times two.

Why *do* my buttons have to match?
Why *can't* I have a mismatched batch?

Who says it's always good and right
to stick with disks of black or white?

And does it really matter, size wise,
if we can buttonhole and resize?

(Don't get me started on the collar
of my shirt or coat or sweater.

I think that they could also gain from
changes in my style and then some.)

Let's trade things out in lots of ways.
Let's mix and match and celebrate

how different things make life more fun.
Let's start with buttons, one by one.

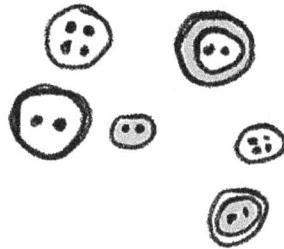

The Wiggle-Waggle Brothers

Two wiggle-waggle boys
on a wiggle-waggle day
went about their business
in a wiggle-waggle way.

They wiggled their four feet
and waggled all their toes.
They laughed and laughed together
as they waggled up their noses.

The wiggle-waggle boys
unfurled a wiggle-waggle map.
They found a wiggly road
and then began to clap.

Let's waggle to the zoo!
they said to one another.
It's a perfect destination!
said the wiggly-waggly brothers.

While there they saw a crocodile
and zebras two-by-two.
They waved at the rhinoceros
and lions. Penguins, too!

They wiggle-waggled home
at the end of that long day—
then the wiggle-waggle boys
knelt down so they could pray.

The wiggles left their bodies
as their Mama sang them tunes
till the wiggle-waggle brothers
fell asleep beneath the moon.

Naptime

Lazy bones! Lazy bones!
What do you think?
Is it time for a nap?
Are your eyes on the brink?

Are you tired? Or sleepy?
Want to go to your room?
Can you read a short book?
Or just plop down to snooze?

Lazy bones! Lazy bones!
I'm tired, too.
If you sleep, then I'll sleep.
Our nap rendezvous!

I Love Me Best

I like to say nice things to me.
I whisper to myself:
You're kind.
You're smart.
You're quite polite.
You're brave and quick.
You're witty!

I also like to tell me *YES*
when *NO* is swirling 'round me.
Why, yes I can!
Yes, please—and thanks!
Yes, I will help—I'm glad to!

I do not like it very much
when people criticize me
in ways that make me feel that they
are trying to capsize me.

That's when I reach into myself
to find what really matters:
I'm kind.
I'm smart.
I'm quite polite.
I'm brave and quick.
I'm witty!

Go Fishin'

Today is a day—
not a regular day—
or a daydream day—
or a horseplay day—
or a do-nothing day—
or a laze around day—
or a getaway day.

It could be Monday—
maybe Tuesday—
might be Wednesday—
even Thursday—
what about Friday—
probably Saturday—
less likely Sunday.

Today is a day—
it's a fine, fine day—
a misty morning day—
a day for me—
a day for you—
a day when we
go fishin'.

My Two Dogs

I have two dogs—they bark at me—
they make a fearsome racket.
They howl and yowl incessantly
until I stop to pat them.

They settle down—these grouchy mates—
while I resume my bustle.
I spring—I dash—I dart—I skate
(which takes a bit of hustle).

And that, in turn, leads to their growls
and bids for more attention.
I tell them *Stop your caterwaul!*
You're adding to my tension!

When darkness falls, I take a rest
and sink into my rocker.
I lean far back—my dogs at last—
stretched out—toes up—no squawking.

Delicious

Cookies, pies, and cakes—
concoctions that I bake—
are fun to make—
and they do taste…
YUMMY!

First I mush the butter—
with eggs, vanilla, sugar—
I sift some flour—
add baking soda…
STIRRING!

I turn the oven on—
then pop confections in—
they start to bake—
I pause and wait…
SALIVATING!

In the cooking gap—
twixt batter, bake, and sup—
apples—plums—
fruity fun…
DELICIOUS!

She Can Be President, Too

She's tall—he's short. He's thin—she's round.
His eyes are blue and hers are brown.

Her skin is sort of multicolored—
and his looks like a pat of butter.

His hair is fair and hers is dark.
In looks they're really miles apart.

But all those outward traits and features
are not enough to make a leader.

Leaders need to have charisma
and compassion, wit, and wisdom.

Intellect goes hand-in-hand
for those who take a high command.

And some reflection must be given
to selfless service as a mission.

In short, the bottom line is clear
that looks are just a thin veneer

when qualities that really matter
lie deep inside aspiring daughters.

So here's to women—old and young—
and girls who also want to run—

for president of our great nation.
Let's lift them up! Let's celebrate them!

Writing Nonsense

Blurble. Slubble. Galuchable, too.
I'm writing nonsense in a gluey word stew.
But what of real words that tangle and twist
in my mouth—on my tongue—past my fast-moving lips?
Think of festoon—or curmudgeon—bamboozle—
it flabbergasts me in my rational noodle.
The conundrum—and then some—as I've come to see it
is my wish to create a believable treatise
that perambulates my cerebellum toward meanings
with no lollygagging or sharp-wit convening.
I've finally decided to skip nonsense words
in favor of phrases that shape clever blurbs
into letters that stick like a ship's gooseneck barnacle—
with occasional *zazoo's* and whoops of *refarnacles.*

Could We Be Friends?

My fuzzy kitten crouches down
with impish eyes aglitter.
She sheathes her claws beneath soft paws
while speaking with a chitter.

I wonder what she sees outside
to make her so excited.
I press my chin against the pane
and outward shine my flashlight.

Imagine my surprise when I
see luminescent glowing
from two red orbs within whose form
a black-masked face is showing.

Raccoon! I whisper to my cat
while trembling she continues.
The small raccoon—herself a cub—
creeps closer to the window.

It reaches out to touch the glass
while my cat noses forward.
With some concern I hesitate
as these two kittens ponder

the eyes and mouths and ears and paws—
an almost mirror image.
Could we be friends? they seem to ask.
Let's try! It takes a village!

Moon Gazing

I am standing outside feeling small and alone
when a firefly blinks near my nose.
It's a startling sight to see twinkling lights
when the darkness is in full repose.

Then a jingle of bells shivers out of the woods
in a racket I know is not birds.
Spring Peepers—I'm told—make that music so bold
when shadows are muffling my words.

What's that sound in the forest? A barking, I think.
Coyotes have come out to play.
They yip and they yap—a cacophony that
I enjoy when it's far, far away.

The clouds overhead slowly part to reveal
the one thing I have wanted to see.
It's a Strawberry Moon in its full perfect bloom
set adrift in the sky to float free.

I bask in its shine in a world that's alive
in ways that I never did know
every day when I play as the sun takes its run
in a half-circle arc of rainbow.

I understand now that the night is alight
with creatures I mostly don't notice.
They're out there. I'm inside. But I'll join them sometimes
when the luminous night draws my focus.

Reduplication

In a busy-whizzy city
on a ziggy-zaggy street
live a happy-scrappy boy
and his silly-willy brother
with their lovey-dovey parents
and a fuzzy-wuzzy cat.

They grow healthy-wealthy veggies
in their itty-bitty garden
so the jibber-jabber boys
have some yummy-yummy food
for their tippy-toppy tummies
and their quick-evolving brains.

In their hustle-bustle days
they read many-many books,
play their clicky-clacky music,
go on pitter-patter hikes,
take their splishy-splashy baths,
and then they say goodnight.

How to Make a Grumpy Boy Smile

How deep is the ocean?
How high is the sky?
How can I make this grumpy boy smile?

Can I read him a story?
Can I sing him a song?
Can I ring a big bell with an extra-loud bong?
Oh! How can I turn that frown upside down
on the face of this boy who lives in this town?

I know, said the boy as he put on his shoes.
Just give me a mallet and other small tools.
I'll line up my wrenches. I'll play with the pliers.
I'll chisel and hammer and cut up some wires.

Then suddenly I saw his mouth start to quiver.
A smile lit his face (and it quite made me shiver).

Now I know what I can do when my Grandson
is grumpy or crabby or hankers for new fun.
I'll give him a toolbox and then with a nod
he'll smile back at me. *LOOK!* The boy that I love.

The Girl with the Bow in Her Hair

I rise every morning—my head full of hair
that's tangled and mangled and making me scared.

My brush and my comb are both frightened, too
at the thought of the job that we know we must do.

We stand at the mirror (my brush, comb, and me)
and we stare at my hair as it tries to break free

from the place where it lives on the top of my head
as it gives not a thought to cute stylings instead.

I take a deep breath—put on my fierce face
(the one that I save for occasions like this).

Then I lift up my hands—place both on my pelt—
and I smooth and I coax till resolve starts to melt.

Why bother with taming this wild silly hairdo
when every new day it turns into a corkscrew?

Then suddenly I have a brilliant idea
of something that maybe can fix my dilemma.

I run to the closet to find the big box
that's filled to the brim with gift-wrapping stuff.

Inside is a bow that's intended to grace
a present for someone who now is unnamed.

I rummage around till I find a red bow—
plop it onto my hair till it nestles just so.

I look in the mirror and grin back at me.
All that hair. Big red bow. I am lov-er-a-lee!

A Fabulous Day

Skinned knees—
a bump on the head—
a little stubbed toe—
and mold on my bread.

Could it be—is it true—
Ouch! I just poked my eye!—
when I jumped from my bed
was it from the wrong side?

Can I restart this day?
Can I change my bad luck?
On a day when the day
is all wrapped up in muck.

I return to my room—
hop onto my mattress—
slide under the covers—
and yelp out *My goodness!*

My best lucky stone that
I keep in my pocket
was tucked in my bed with
my books and toy rocket.

I scoop it up quickly—
I snug it away—
I skip out the door—
it's a fabulous day!

Kale Salad

I love kale salad. Yes, I do.
I love the way it sticks like glue
to mashed potatoes on my plate.
I swirl them up. They taste so great!

Avocados also are my
go-to treats when I am hungry.
Smashed on toast or served up plain—
they're green—they're good—they feed my brain.

Don't get me started praising beets.
To me, they are a favorite treat.
And what of broccoli? Okra? Carrots?
In soup or stew—they all have merit.

I only draw a line on veggies
with one food that makes me edgy.
That's asparagus. It's true!
It makes me shudder when I chew.

But for the rest—
please serve them up.
I'll try and taste—
they're all good grub.

Pen, Pencil, or Crayon?

For my money, I must say
I'd rather use a pen
to write a card or simple note
to family and to friends.

There are others in my sphere
who much prefer a pencil
when scratching down a fleeting thought
that might demand erasure.

Some acceptance must be shared
for those who write with crayon.
They choose their colors carefully:
blue or green or orange.

They are brave souls who do believe
that coloring is truly
the way to show the world aglow
in all its vivid beauty.

Now I ask you for your thoughts
to choose twixt pen or pencil.
Or are you just a scallywag
who colors life like tinsel?

A Voice Clear and True

Chirp! Chirp! trilled a warbly voice from the tree—
If you look toward the sky, that's where you'll see me!

So the small boy named Peter stood up on his tiptoes—
he looked and he gazed till his eyes spied a sparrow.

He blew her a kiss then turned with a swoosh—
Buzz! Buzz! came a sound from out of the bush.

I'm landing on petals! I'm slurping up nectar!
the buzzy words droned from the honey collector.

Peter ran to the hedges—he peered at the posies—
at last a big bumble flew up from the roses.

He reached out his hands with his fingers spread wide
to touch the bee's wings—then a twig snapped. Surprise!

Lucy! Sweet Lucy was starting to prowl
on her kitty-cat paws—making shy, fretful meows.

I'm hungry. I'm tired. I'm sleepy. I'm crabby.
came the querulous voice of the little gray tabby.

But Peter was thoughtful and gentle and kind—
and Lucy—who loved him—never did mind

when he patted her head or snuggled up close—
so she waited and paused as they stretched to bump noses.

Peter cradled his cat and the bird swooped on high
and the bumble he bumbled across the blue sky.

Then the boy finally spoke with a voice clear and true—
I love you! I love you! Cat...bird...bumble, too!

Practicing Yoga

I'm a volcano—a waterfall, too—
when I'm practicing yoga in my living room.

Now I'm a crane—see me reach up so high.
A stork—then an eagle. I take a swan dive.

Animals wild I can pose with my body.
Look at me! I'm a bear. And I breathe like a lion.

Domesticate animals are nothing new
when I am a cat or a dog or a…MOO!

When I want to slow down, I crouch into rabbit—
or grab my two feet—happy baby's my gambit.

I choose what I want when I practice my yoga.
It's good for all children. Come! Join me in cobra!

Murky

The weather girl stands inside the TV,
forecasting unstoppable weather.
Murky today—and tomorrow, she says,
will be drizzly and drear beyond measure.

I think I might cry at her cheeky bright smile
and predictions of gloomy horizons.
Give me sunshine instead and warm temps overhead—
(that's my prayer for a change in the season).

Still, I'm stuck in the muck of this nor'easter rut
of dim days that bring dank, drenching rainfall.
I must weather this weather from inside my house
reading books—drinking tea—wearing sweaters.

The Galloping Garbage Truck

The galloping garbage truck rumbles along
at a pace that is truly alarming.
It zooms down the road—pausing only at curbs—
in a dash for the trash with no warnings.

I wait for the truck on my porch where the view
gives a perfect perspective for watching
as it drives house to house—announcing itself
with a burp then a blare and a coughing.

The sounds make me laugh and the binman I see
gives a nod when I smile his direction.
As he dumps all our stuff in the back of the truck,
I clap loud and he grins with affection.

Though no words do we share, we're a well-suited pair—
the lorryman and his admirer.
I can picture my march to the green machine's perch—
taking charge—steering far—as the driver.

My parents have other ideas for me—
transportation is one of their visions.
I could pilot a plane—engineering the same.
Astronaut? Build a yacht? My decision.

But for now I'm content to salute my new friend
every Tuesday when he comes a-calling.
We smile, wave, and laugh over everyone's trash.
It's a job. He works hard. I'm applauding.

Stars

Here's to stars—celestial orbs—
those incandescent lights.
Cloudless nights do they ignite
the sky with glints of white.

I want to board a rocket ship
bound for the Milky Way.
I'll fly past constellations
living in our galaxy.

I'll search for Little Dipper
and follow her North Star.
I'll contemplate Orion
who hunts from near and far.

At last, I'll land upon the moon
ashine in astral glory.
I'll turn to gaze through all those stars
at Earth—my home—my aerie.

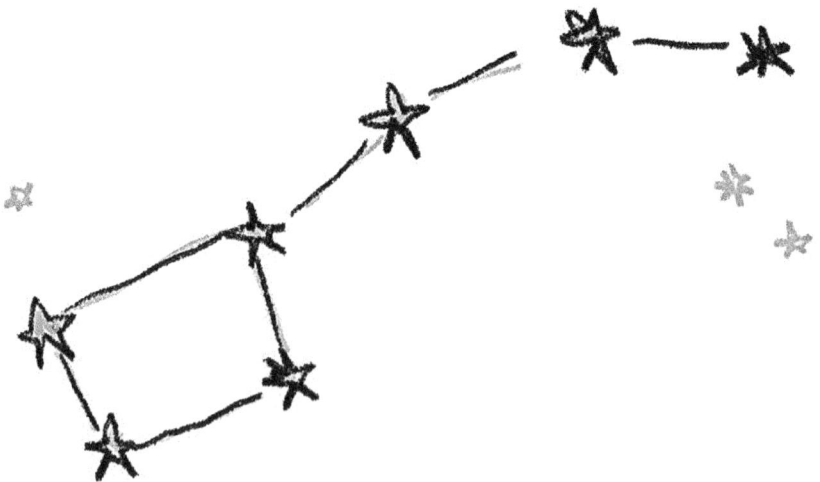

A Herd of Turtles in a Cloud of Heifer Dust

In a race with some cows—
whose quick pace slowly slows—
is a sea turtle bale creeping forward.

They blunder along in
a headstrong response to
the charm of the water they're seeking.

As the bovine stampede
loses steam (dwindling lead)
a reptilian win seems more likely.

The turtles march on while
the cows pause to munch on
sweet clover that ever does tempt them.

It's that ill-advised move
that gives turtles a groove
for the win—now they grin—in their triumph.

These cunning shelled warriors—
fine as frog's fur and glorious—
ashine in the gleam of the morning.

They know one small thing—
their advantage to win—
stretch your neck—don't look back—keep on going.

My Balloon

My balloon
was very fine—
I loved it
in my way.
It was
bright red—
it had
a thread
so never
would it
stray.
One sunny
morn
I took it out
so we
could stroll
around.
It glanced
up high
where it
did spy
a lovely
yellow
crown.
The shining
sun
beguiled
my friend
to join it
in its romp.
My red balloon
then tugged
and pulled
until the string
I dropped.

Before I
had a chance
to snag
the tether
back to me,
it swiftly rose
beyond
my grasp
then gently
flew
away.

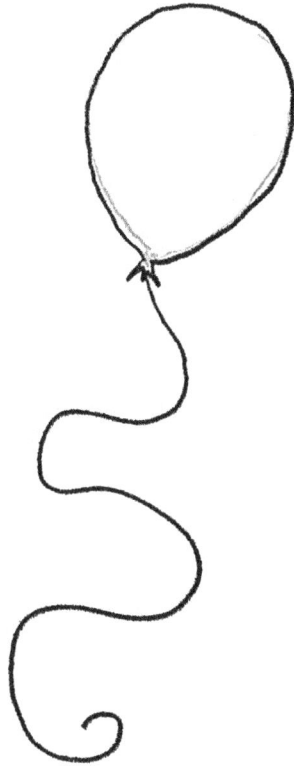

Glossary

Aerie—A large nest for a bird of prey
Aspiring—Desiring and working to achieve a specific goal
Astral—Connected with or resembling stars
Bamboozle—To trick someone
Barnacle—A marine crustacean that attaches itself to surfaces
Beguiled—To charm or enchant someone
Blunder—A careless mistake
Blurble—An invented, nonsensical word
Blurbs—A short description (often of a book or movie)
Bovine—Relating to cows or oxen
Cacophony—A harsh, discordant mixture of sounds
Caterwaul—Long, wailing cries, screeches, or howls
Celestial—Related to the sky or outer space
Cerebellum—A part of the brain located in the back of the head
Charisma—Attractiveness or charm
Confection—A dish or delicacy made with sweet ingredients
Constellations—A group of stars forming a recognizable pattern
Contemplate—To think about
Conundrum—A confusing, difficult problem or question
Convening—To bring together in a group
Corkscrew—Shaped in a spiral
Curmudgeon—A bad-tempered (often old) person
Domesticate—To tame an animal
Edible—Suitable for eating
Festoon—To decorate with a chain that hangs between two points
Flabbergast—To shock or surprise
Galaxy—Billions of stars held together by gravitational attraction
Galloping—Running or moving forward quickly
Galuchable—An invented, nonsensical word
Gambit—An action that is intended to gain an advantage
Gooseneck—Something that is curved like the neck of a goose
Hankers—Yearns or longs for
Impish—Doing slightly naughty things for fun
Incandescent—Emitting light as a result of heating
Little Dipper—A ladle-shaped part of the Ursa Minor constellation

Lollygagging—To dawdle or spend time aimlessly
Lorryman/Binman—British for garbageman
Luminescent—A spontaneous emission of light
Luminous—Full of bright, shining light, especially in the dark
Milky Way—The spiral galaxy that contains Earth's solar system
Noodle—Slang for head or brain
Nor'easter—A storm formed along North America's eastern coast
North Star—The northern hemisphere star toward which
  the Earth's axis points (aka Polestar)
Orb—Something circular
Orion—A constellation resembling a hunter with belt and sword
Pelt—An animal's fur
Perambulate—To walk about
Querulous—Complaining in a whining manner
Rational—Something that is based on reason or logic
Reduplication—A word-forming process that repeats all
  or part of a word
Refarnacle—An invented, nonsensical word
Rendezvous—Meeting at an agreed-upon time and place
Repose—A state of rest or sleep
Salivate—To drool
Scallywag—A scamp or rascal
Sheathe—To cover something
Slubble—An invented, nonsensical word
Strawberry Moon—The full moon in June that is closest
  to the summer solstice
Tranquil—Calm
Treatise—A written work
Unfurl—To open
Zazoo—An invented, nonsensical word

About the Author

Pamela R. Anderson is a traveler, blues music lover, yoga practitioner, and former public radio fundraiser who grew up in Ohio's Steel Valley. Her chapbook *Just the Girls: A Kaleidoscope of Butterflies; A Drift of Honeybees* was published by The Poetry Box in 2020; Finishing Line Press published her chapbook *Widow Maker* in 2021. Much of her writing focuses on the Holocaust and her father's WWII service in the 82nd Airborne; her Holocaust poem "My Brother's Coat" won an AWP Intro Journals Project award. Anderson's poetry has appeared in *JennyMag.org, Atticus Review, Volney Road Review,* and elsewhere. She is a graduate of the NEOMFA Program.

www.pamelaranderson.org
@prandersonpoet